TELL ME ABOUT YOURSELF

A Journey to Discover and Embrace the
Real YOU

Noella M. Mbulapey

PUBLISHERS

ISBN: 978-1-958443-43-9 (paperback)

DEDICATION

First and foremost, I would like to give thanks to God Almighty for allowing me to be His vessel to write this book. This book is a pure product of obedience. I wrote it while going through one of the hardest seasons of my life. At times I gave up on it and thought I just needed to focus on myself, until the Holy Spirit reminded me that obedience was the key to unlock God's blessings and favor upon our lives.

I would also like to thank my biological parents, Valentin Bope and Jacqueline Pelenge, who trained me in God's ways. Even though life was not always fair, and they are not perfect, they made sure I grew up with values and morals grounded in the Word of God. Paul said, *"I have planted, Apollos watered; but God gave the increase." (1 Corinthians 3:6 - KJV).* God may have used different people to help me grow, but He used them to plant the seed by teaching me the fundamentals of

Christian life. My parents did not only help me know God, but they also taught me moral lessons that I still stand by and apply today. My dad always pushed us to be men and women of integrity and responsible in all ways.

My mother has been—and still is—my strongest intercessor. She believed in me and in who God called me to be even before I made my entrance into the land of the living. When she was pregnant with me, she received a prophetic word that I would be a servant of God. She believed in that prophecy and did her best to see my life in its fulfillment. Against all odds, she decided to give birth to me, and for that, I will forever be grateful.

I would also like to dedicate this book to my spiritual father, Dr. Rod Parsley, for showing me how to love God and His people by example. I know God has granted me the boldness of John the Baptist when it comes to preaching; however, I became a lot bolder when it comes to preaching the Gospel, even the most sensitive topics, once I started serving under him. I thank you for your love and leadership.

Last but not least, special thanks to my biological siblings, to all my mentees and members of Esther Generation Ministries, to my church family at World Harvest Church and to the amazing people, mentors, and friends who have pushed me to write this book—some of them without even realizing it—Kai Howard, Yolanda and Chris Degen, Erica Howard, Josue Asani. Ritha Mwidya Wa Shakapanga, Shekina Kabeya Useni, and many more.

TABLE OF CONTENTS

INTRODUCTION

I remember my first job interview. I did some research on Google the night before on the possible questions an interviewer would ask me. I clicked on every link that said "interview questions and answers." While looking at the answers, I was also figuring out how I could adjust them to make them more personal. However, one question came often that captured my attention: "Tell me about yourself." I looked at the question for a few minutes, searching for an answer. It was my first interview, and I was not used to it. I started to draft an answer. I began with my name, what I was doing at school, my background, etc.

Although I mentioned all this, I was not quite satisfied with my answer. The question was just asking about my identity; normally, it shouldn't be that hard to answer, right? Well, if you could see the confusion on my face, I wasn't quite close to getting it. I decided to look at the answers that the article suggested. They were other people's answers, but I did not know how to respond to that question, so I copied and memorized them word for word.

The next day was my interview. You could tell how frustrated I was that I even forgot to take my breakfast. I kept on repeating the answers I had memorized. Yes, you read it well; I memorized an identity, not mine, but some unknown people online. I prayed and left my apartment, dressed like a lady who worked at a bank, with my hair in a ponytail. As people would say; dress how you want to be addressed. You could tell I was ready for that position, and it was not at a bank. I applied to be a server at a local restaurant.

I finally got there. I was in a small meeting room, facing my interviewer and smiling like a little girl who just opened her Christmas gift. Then he opened his mouth and the first thing that came out was, "Tell me about yourself." I froze for a few seconds but still maintained eye contact to not make him think I was scared, but deep inside, I wanted to cry. Then, I started repeating what I had memorized. He seemed impressed with my answer, even though those qualities I mentioned were not mine.

The interview went well, and the manager promised to call me back if they wanted to move forward with my application. I went home, and my friend and roommate asked me how it went. I said it was good, but my facial expression was saying otherwise. I was not happy with what I did. Questions started haunting me. I kept asking myself, "Who are you, woman?"

Normally, at this point, I should have been worried about how the interview went and if I would get the job or not. Nevertheless, that was by far the least of my concerns. I kept thinking about that question and how I should have answered it in my own words. Although the question might have been asked in another context to allow me to market myself for the position I applied for, I felt ashamed for not being able to figure out my identity, to tell myself who I was.

Moments later, I started comforting myself by saying I was young. I had just entered my twenties. I hadn't learned much about life, so it was normal to not know who I was. Once I grew up and got more experience, I would be able to describe myself. However, it was not quite normal.

I believe that in every stage of our lives, we should know how to describe ourselves no matter how old we are or what level of experience we have. Each stage of our lives is a piece of a puzzle; a part of the big picture of who we become. The statement might be improved as we get older, but we should have a basic knowledge of our identity, a foundation we are building our lives on.

Identity, by definition, is the qualities, beliefs, personality traits, appearances, and expressions that characterize a person. In this book, I would like to approach the notion of identity, especially as children of God.

Although the question "Tell Me About Yourself" was related to a job position, while analyzing the question with the Biblical perspective and observing the world we live in right

" What keeps us from growing into becoming a better version of ourselves is the fact that we are content with how things are now, and we give reasons for not wanting more and better. "

#TMAY

now, I came to understand that so many people don't really know who they are. They don't know their "real" identity. People either define themselves in comparison to what they see in other people or even on the internet—social media, to be more specific. Others even adjust themselves to the circumstances they are facing. I have no money in my account, therefore I am poor. I can't give birth, therefore I am barren. No man or woman seems to be attracted to me, therefore I am ugly. I failed my classes, therefore I am not smart. People rejected me, therefore I am not a good person. The situation you face should not determine your identity. If you find yourself in that equation, you are among the people I wrote this book for. Keep on reading.

CHAPTER 1
CREATED IN GOD'S IMAGE

One day I bought a printer. When opening the box, I saw everything I needed to turn it on: the power cord, ink bottles, a CD, and the printer itself. However, I did not know at first what to do to get the printer working. I started figuring out what to do. I spent thirty minutes on Google and YouTube, watching videos of people who had purchased the same product. After a while, I still did not know how to turn it on and just decided to do it later.

When I was standing up, I flipped the box and noticed a piece of paper falling on the floor. That paper was a letter sent from the manufacturer explaining how his product works and how it should be operated. It was the printer user's manual. I followed the instructions and got everything done in less than five minutes. Things would have been easier if I started from the manual instead of searching elsewhere.

As children of God, if we really want to know our identity, we need to go back to our Creator. Genesis 1:27 says, *"So God created man in his own image, in the image of God created him; male and female He created them." (NKJV)*. Our identity is defined by God Himself. Who we are is related to who He is and what He says about us. Identity is an important factor in both the spiritual realm and in the society we live in. Who we are will determine how people treat us and to what level they will place us. Who we are will also determine our influence in the spiritual realm because our authority is the knowledge we have about ourselves. A prince who is not aware of his status and who is living like an ordinary man might as well be treated as ordinary. This is why the Bible says in Psalm 82:6-7, *"I said, "You are gods, and all of you are children of the Most High. But you shall die like men, and fall like one of the princes."" (NKJV)*. Not knowing who you are is setting yourself up for defeat.

When we ask about identity, people often define themselves according to the situations they have lived or are currently living in. A woman who has been married for five years with no kids will call herself barren; a man who has cancer will present himself as the sickness he carries in his body; yet, the Bible says, *"Let the weak say I am strong"* (see Joel 3:10). This is paradoxical, right? He is weak; how can God tell him to say he is strong? Weak and strong are two completely opposite adjectives. God's truth does not always have to be

14

" Who we are will determine how people treat us and to what level they will place us. **"**

#TMAY

logical to human understanding. His Word does not always follow the norms set by the world.

When one wants to understand how a printer works, they need to read the manual. The same thing applies to human beings.

I spent thirty minutes figuring out how to turn a printer on, while, in fact, it should have only taken me five minutes. This applies to real life. We are searching for answers elsewhere when the solution is just before our eyes. People are looking for other ways of embracing life to define who they should be, and that alone is the root of a lot of frustration and also a waste of time. Just because it took someone five years to build a business does not mean it should take the same amount of time for you to build one. Maybe in how God orchestrated things for your life it should only take you one year, but you don't know that because you did not read the manual: the Word of God. You are busy living a life of comparison.

Through His Word, God is just teaching us to set aside our view of ourselves, how we perceive ourselves, how we feel in our body, the situation we live in, or even how people view us. Our identity is not found in what we go through or what we experience but in who He created us to be and what His Word says about us. He is the only one who has the right to define us according to His Word.

Remember, early in this chapter, I spoke about the printer that came with a manual, right? See yourself as that printer, God as the manufacturer, and His Word as the manual. He gave us His Word to help us live the life He intended us to live before creation. Even more, His Word became flesh so that we don't only have a book to read but a Man to live by; the perfect example to follow.

A few years ago, I had to fly to Atlanta, Georgia for my best friend's baby shower. The week before my flight, on a Thursday evening, when I got home, I realized that I left my wallet at the work office. My schedule was hybrid. I worked Monday and Friday from home and Tuesday to Thursday from the office. So, basically, I was not supposed to go to the office the next day; not until the following Tuesday. I could go there and pick it up myself, but who would drive thirty minutes with GPA-looking gas prices? Not me for sure. We all needed that gas price to look like an academic probation at some point. The gas price was so high that people could only drive when necessary. I wished I could use a bike to go to work. As a result, I called my manager and let him know about my situation. He suggested sending my wallet via post and promised that I would get it the next day or any time before my flight. The day after, I had not received my wallet yet. My flight date was approaching, and all my IDs were in my wallet.

I pray that God helps you see yourself through His eyes as you read this book.

I started stressing out, calling the post office, and they told me the estimated arrival date. Guess what? The wallet would arrive the day after my flight. I couldn't miss that event for nothing in the world. She was my best friend. We had been there for each other in all the major events of our lives; birthdays, graduation, wedding, and now she was carrying my baby girl. So, I started doing some research on how I could travel with no ID whatsoever. I was seated in my car when I remembered that I had my EAD card in the glove compartment. "Thank God!" I shouted. That was my last resort, but I needed to make sure I was allowed to travel with it. So, I called the airline and asked. The agent told me as long as it had my picture on it, I should be fine.

Our identity is not found in what we experience in life but in what God created us to be.

I took you on this journey so you see one thing: the airport needed my image to identify me. My identity depended not only on the name on the EAD card but on my image. My face had to be there. Your name might be man-given, but your image is how God created you.

This is what happened in Genesis 1:27. By creating us in His image, God gave us His identity. He gave us His power and authority so we can rule on earth. You are the mirror through which God sees Himself. The Bible says, *"As He is, so are we in this world."* (see 1 John 4:17). We are the reflection of God

18

on earth. Nevertheless, as children of God, we fail to understand this because of several things: we either lack knowledge or the knowledge we have is distorted. I pray that through this book, you fully understand your identity by the revelation of the Holy Spirit. I pray that God enlightens you and opens your eyes so you can see you through Him.

Your name might be man-given, but your image is how God created you.

CHAPTER 2
THE RIGHT ENVIRONMENT

The identity we received from God at creation gives us the capacity and the ability to perform like God on earth. It gave man the authority and power to dominate. Genesis 1:28 says: *Then God blessed them, and God said to them, "Be fruitful and multiply; fill the earth and subdue it; have dominion over the fish of the sea, over the birds of the air, and over every living thing that moves on the earth." (Genesis 1:28 - NKJV).* Identity always comes before authority. The less you know about yourself, the more limited you will be in using the full potential inside of you. The Bible says in Genesis 2 that after God created Adam and Eve, He then created an environment in which they could use what He placed in them. God created Eden and placed them in there so they could take care of it and rule over everything. Both man and woman had the privilege to be consistently in the presence of God and were given authority over other creatures. Eden was the perfect place a man could live in and be who he was created to be.

You may ask yourself why you have not developed your full potential. "Why am I not blooming in what I do?" One possibility is that you are still confused about your identity, or you haven't discovered who you truly are at all. You may be out of Eden, out of the presence of God, away from Him. I pray that from wherever you have gone, no matter how far, you come back to His presence, which is the safest environment that can allow you to grow and discover your true self. Come back to the place where your life gets its full essence and meaning; to the place where He can turn your mess into a world-changing message and your pain into a great purpose.

In the book of Exodus, the Bible speaks of Moses' encounter with God through a burning bush. When God told Moses about the assignment he had to fulfill, which was bringing the people of Israel out of Egypt, Moses asked God, "Who am I?" implying that he was not that good to trust him with this task. Moses may have thought his background did not qualify him for that mission. God's answer was not "You are Moses, the murderer." Yes, Moses killed an Egyptian after he saw him beating a Hebrew (see Exodus 2:11). God didn't say, "You are Moses, the adopted Israelite who grew up in a foreign land." God said, "I will be with you." (see Exodus 3:12). The presence of God was all Moses needed to become who God wanted him to be despite all his weaknesses, trauma, pain, and rejection.

22

Like Moses, your identity is not what you have been through, what you have or have not done, or what you have accomplished in life, whether good or bad. Your identity is found in WHO is with you; whose presence you walk with. We see the same scenario in Judges 6. God asked Gideon to save Israel out of Midian's hand.

Identity comes before authority, and authority is contingent to territories.

"So he said to Him, "O my Lord, how can I save Israel? Indeed my clan is the weakest in Manasseh, and I am the least in my father's house." And the Lord said to him, "Surely I will be with you, and you shall defeat the Midianites as one man."" *(Judges 6:15-16 - NKJV)*. See, this is what we all do. We bring forth our weaknesses, inabilities, and past when we face our purpose. Like Moses and Gideon, we limit ourselves based on our experience. God doesn't see your past mistakes, family background, and the things you have endured. He sees you based on what He put inside of you; His *Ruah*, His power. The Lord replied to Gideon, "I will be with you, and you will strike down all the Midianites, leaving none alive." (see Judges 6:16). God's presence is all you need to be who you need to be. Gideon discovered that he could accomplish a lot more than he thought just by having God on his side. Now my questions to you are: *"Whose side are you on? Who or what is leading your life right now? Who are you surrounded by?"*

The presence of God is not as far as you think; He is already in you. The Holy Spirit is dwelling inside of you. Romans 8:11 says, *"The same Spirit that raised Jesus from the dead lives in you..." (NKJV)*. The fact is, just because He lives in you doesn't mean you allow Him to work. Some of us have Jesus in our homes, but we have placed Him in the attic. He is in the house, but where? What position is He occupying? What importance have we given Him? Maybe it is time for you to let Him take control of your life and destiny again. Maybe it is time for you to let Him define you again. Maybe it is time for you to surrender and come back to Him again.

The Bible says in Job 32:8, *"But there is a spirit in man; and the breath of the Almighty gives him understanding." (NKJV)*. The Spirit of God in you will give you an understanding about your identity.

"In the same way, the Spirit helps us in our weakness... He who searches our hearts knows the mind of the Spirit because the Spirit intercedes for God's people in accordance with the will of God." (Romans 8:26-27 – NIV).

The Holy Spirit is a Friend who understands your frustrations and confusion right now. He knows what you have been through, and He is ready to help. Listen, you are not responsible for how life has treated you so far, but you are responsible for making a change today. Say this prayer with me:

> *Holy Spirit of God, I come before You today, and I surrender myself, my will, my desires, my pain, my*

struggles, my guilt, my weaknesses, my trauma, my insecurities, and my confusion unto You. From today on, I give You total control of my life. Lead me to the path of righteousness for God's glory. Help me become not what the world or myself see but who God sees in me, in Jesus' name. Amen.

" *Listen, you are not responsible for how life has treated you so far, but you are responsible for making a change today.* **"**

#TMAY

Use this space below to write down the areas of your life where you need the total control of God. This is called a "surrender list."

_____

_____

_____

_____

_____

_____

Although being in the presence of God is important, we live on earth, meaning, whether we like it or not, we are called to deal with humanity. God never created man to be alone. Genesis 2:18 says, *And the Lord God said, "It is not good that man should be alone; I will make him a helper comparable to him." (NKJV)*. God gave Adam a helper, Eve. He intended for us to need each other and live in community.

The people we surround ourselves with have a direct impact on us. The effect can be positive or negative. When we are born, the first environment we are subject to is family: parents, siblings, cousins, grandparents, uncles, aunties, nephews, nieces, and so on. When children

A community is a group of people who share something in common; it can be a language, culture, traditions, goals, mindset, etc.

are born, they are like wet clay. They can be molded into any shape because they adjust themselves to what they see and hear. Children learn by imitating adults.

I remember watching a video on the internet of a three-year-old boy who was preaching with a remote in his hand, substituting for the mic. I went to the page, and I realized that the boy's dad was a pastor. Basically, the little boy was doing what he saw his dad do on a regular basis. The first identity a child adopts comes from the environment he or she grows up in. This is why it is important for parents to set the right examples and make sure their children grow up surrounded by the right people.

Besides family, another environment we can be influenced by is school. This is where family education continues; nevertheless, that education can either be improved or deteriorate. Children get to meet friends and interact with them. In that interaction, there is an exchange of different habits depending on each child's educational background. This is when you notice that your child, for example, who never cursed in his life, one day comes back from school with cursing words coming out of his mouth. The type of friends he hangs out with has a direct or indirect influence on him.

This is why the Bible says in Proverbs 22:6, *"Train up a child in the way he should go, and when he is old he will not depart from it." (NKJV)*. Parents, whether biological, adoptive or anyone, taking care of a child should show them their identity through the Word of God so that later, when they are confronted with negative environments, they will not be influenced and acquire an identity that is not theirs. The different environments we live in shape us.

Now ask yourself these questions, *Who am I surrounded by? Am I surrounded by people who bring value to my life? Am I surrounded by people who are led by the Holy Ghost and by the Word of God?* If you can't answer yes to these questions, then it is time you start reevaluating your standards and know who is fit to be in your close circle. In fact, some of us do not have circles but cages. Anything that does not help you be better and reach your purpose in God is actually a prison. A friend who does not bring you closer to God is actually drawing you farther from your purpose and destiny. 1 Corinthians 15:33 says, *"Do not be deceived: "Evil company corrupts good habits.""* *(NKJV).* It does not matter how good of a person you are. It does not matter how good your intentions might be; if you have the wrong people in your circle, they will drag you down to their level; to who they are and what they think.

> *You should always evaluate your surroundings and know who is fit to be in your close circle.*

Here are a few questions to help you know if your relationships—friends and family—are healthy for your life and, most importantly, your Christian journey: *"What is your relationship built on? God or the world? Do they push you towards your purpose? Can you trust them to lift you up in prayer in times of need? Are they honest enough to tell you if*

"Who am I surrounded by? Am I surrounded by people who bring value to my life? Am I surrounded by people who are led by the Holy Ghost and by the Word of God?"

#TMAY

you are wrong and how you can better yourself? Do they value you for your qualities and not just emphasize your weaknesses?"

May God give you the discernment to know who you can connect yourself to. You should be surrounded by people who have the fear of God; people who will help you accomplish the mission God has given you; people who will be prayer partners; people who have God's Word as a foundation and reference. I want you to say this prayer with me:

Heavenly Father, help me discern Your voice and follow Your lead in the relationships I create in my life. Bless me with people who see me as You see me and support me in becoming the best version of myself. Help me associate myself with wise people so I can attain wisdom; as the Bible says, "Walk with the wise and become wise, associate with fools and get in trouble." (Proverbs 13:20). Separate me from what and who separates me from You. Remove every relationship that is ruling over my relationship with You. As I pray to be surrounded by good people, help me be a good person others should be surrounded by as well, in Jesus' name. Amen.

CHAPTER 3
THE TRUTH TWISTER

One of the greatest battles men have on earth is the fight against the knowledge of one's identity; the knowledge of who God called him to be or do. Always remember this, the enemy will always come to tell you who you are not or make you doubt who God says you truly are.

In Genesis 3, after God created both man and woman and after He established them in the garden of Eden, we see an intruder come in. The people you surround yourself with matter. You may have been in a good season for a while, and just getting the wrong person in your circle can ruin everything.

Genesis 3:1 says, *"Now the serpent was more cunning than any beast of the field which the Lord God had made. And he said to the woman, "Has God indeed said, 'You shall not eat of every tree of the garden'?" (NKJV).* Satan, at first, did not add any new information. He came to attest what Eve already knew; however, his attestation came as a question, "Did God really say?" This is what he does with us. You are failing your classes now: "Did God really say you would get your degree?" Cancer has gotten to the last phase now and the doctor says you have a 2% chance of making it: "Did God really say you would be healed?" This is your fifth failed relationship: "Did God really say you will get married?" You are facing bankruptcy, and your businesses are crashing: "Did God really say you are blessed beyond measure, in the city and in the field?"

Since COVID-19 started, so many people have faced depression, suicidal thoughts, anxiety, etc., because the devil knows how to play with people's minds to the point where they even forget what God says in His Word. Do not let the devil deceive you. Just because everything is going down out there with the economy and the government doesn't mean that things must go down with you.

Before you become a citizen in your country or your parents' child, you are first and foremost a child of the Most High God. You carry His promises in your life. Don't let a global reality become your personal truth. Just because it is happening in the neighborhood does not mean it should reach your home. The Bible says in Exodus 10:23, *"They did not see one another; nor did anyone rise from his place for three days. But all the*

" You may have been in a good season for a while, and just getting the wrong person in your circle can ruin everything. **"**

#TMAY

children of Israel had light in their dwellings." (NKJV). This word is for you; no matter what is going on out there, Christ is in your boat. No matter how dark the world might be, Jesus is the light, and having Him in your life is all you will ever need.

The devil always comes to distort what God has promised to do with us and what He has said to us. The Bible mentions that Jesus went through forty days and forty nights of prayer and fasting. On the last day, Satan came the same way he did with Eve. His purpose is always to separate men from the presence of God. For those of you who think that the devil is ignorant, it is sad to see that even the devil knows the Bible better than some Christians. One language repeated itself here again: "Wasn't it written?" In other words, "Didn't God really say?"

Luke 4:9-13 says, *The devil led Him (Jesus) to Jerusalem and had Him stand on the highest point of the temple. "If you are the Son of God," he said, "throw yourself down from here. For it is written: "'He will command his angels concerning you to guard you carefully; they will lift you up in their hands, so that you will not strike your foot against a stone.' Jesus answered, "It is said: 'Do not put the Lord your God to the test.'" When the devil had finished all this temptation, he left him until an opportune time." (NIV).* Jesus knew who He was, and He was rooted in the Word of God, so it was impossible for the devil to fool Him. Hosea 4:6 says, *"My people are destroyed for lack of knowledge." (NKJV).* If you don't want to be intimidated by the lies of the devil, you need to be grounded in the truth; you need to read the Word of God.

" Don't let a global reality become your personal truth. Just because it's happening in the neighborhood does not mean it should reach your home. **"**

#TMAY

Remember, the Bible is the manual you were sent with. The Word of God is the truth you should live by.

I speak now against every lie of the devil concerning your life, including your identity, health, finances, family, job, etc., in the name of Jesus Christ. I declare that the Word of God will become your truth.

Some of us are dealing with depression and suicidal thoughts because we let the lies of the devil take precedence over the Word of God. May God set your mind free right now, in Jesus' name. I shut down the voice of the devil in your mind, soul, heart, and spirit, and I increase the volume of the voice of God. I rebuke the spirit of manipulation in any form over your life. I rebuke every truth-twister, whether it is your family, circle of friends, or anyone who has access to you. I cancel the effect of every evil word and lie spoken over your destiny, in Jesus' name. Amen.

CHAPTER 4
EARS, DOORS TO INNER SELF

I want you to understand that one of the biggest tools the devil uses to deceive us is our ears. Yes, you read it right. What you set your ears to hear can dictate the trajectory of your life. Eve made one mistake that caused the generations after her to live lives of hardship. Her mistake was giving her ears to the wrong person. That act influenced not only her identity but made her lose her position in the presence and in the eyes of God.

Now I ask you this question, *"What have you set your ears to?"* Let me ask that question another way, *"Who have you given your ears to? Who do you listen to the most?"*

In Mark 1:24, the Bible tells the story of Jesus in His early ministry. Many did not really know who He was. One day, while preaching and healing, He met a demon who shouted, "I know who You are!" The demon cried out through the man it inhabited that Jesus was "The Holy One of God!" Immediately, Jesus told it to "Be quiet and come out of the man." Did the demon lie? No. He spoke the truth. Jesus is the Holy One of God, so why did Jesus tell him to shut up? The answer is, Jesus was already in a phase in His ministry where people kept on attributing His works to the devil. Consequently, the last thing He wanted was to be introduced by a demon. Jesus knew how demons work and did not want to give them any influence over His ministry.

The devil enjoys changing the image of who we are by using our ears. He attempts to whisper words like "You're a failure" in your ears or "You're irritating, useless, unlovable, pathetic, unforgivable, too much, insufficient, broken, ugly, stupid, worthless…"

The strange thing in the verse we read is that what the demon stated about Jesus was correct. A lie may begin with something genuine, such as a personality quality or a beautiful attribute, but if we listen to it, if we allow even a smidgeon of its power in our lives, the devil will pervert any and every fact to suit his own purposes. The devil needs access to operate in our lives, and he will use any means, even good ones, just to get a space in your heart to get to his plans. He labels our identity with those wicked phrases till we believe that is who we are.

Sometimes, a lie starts with something that is true. When Satan came to Jesus in the desert, he presented Him with the truth; the gospel, the Word of God. However, he twisted the Word of God to suit his own purpose. He did the same thing with Adam and Eve. He twisted the instruction God gave them and, at the end of the game, he won, and they were sent out of the garden. Jesus would never allow demons to define who He is, and neither should you.

The first step is to discipline your ears by filtering the information you receive. What influencer, coach, or motivator do you follow on social media, and what message are they giving? What podcast or radio program do you listen to on your way to work? Does what you are listening to fit what God says about you in His Word? The Bible says that faith comes by hearing, and hearing the Word of God (see Romans 10:17). It means we can also build our belief system on something other than the Word of God.

We should ask ourselves the above questions, especially in this information age we live in where the media has taken the wheel of many people's destinies. We must set boundaries to what we set our ears to. It is time for you to leave those chats where topics do not add anything valuable to your life. It is time to leave those groups that are polluting your mind, spirit, and soul with gossip and slander. It is time to unfollow those pages on social media that are leading you astray.

The reason many marriages are failing is because people choose marriage counselors based on the number of likes and followers. They take advice from people who do not even

"" *Jesus would never allow demons to define who He is, and neither should you.* ""

#TMAY

consider that marriage is first God's institution before it becomes a legal one. We take advice with no discernment at all and destroy our own lives. One of the reproaches that God always gives me as His prophet is to not listen to anybody or anything. As seers or prophets of God, most of the time we communicate with Him through some of the five senses. We hear from Him, we see, smell, and feel things. God spoke to me and said, "I use your spirit to reveal things to you so you can share it with My people. If your spirit is full of immoral things, you will not be able to hear Me clearly and convey the message properly." If you have many voices in your head, it will be difficult to discern the voice of God. Consequently, I try my very best to make sure that anything that does not glorify God does not have access to me, that is, the music I listen to, the movies I watch, the type of content I watch on social media, the things I read on the internet, etc.

Always make sure you feed your mind with the right thing. My prayer for you is that God gives you the strength to say no and set boundaries. As the book says in Zechariah 4:6, *"'Not by might nor by power, but by My Spirit,' Says the Lord of hosts."* *(NKJV)*. I pray that the Holy Spirit gives you the strength to discipline your life according to His Word.

CHAPTER 5
THE WORDS THAT YOU SPEAK, SO SHALL IT BE

In addition to our ears being doors to our inner self, our mouth has the power to either create or dismantle, build or destroy. Genesis 1 says that God created everything with His Word. He spoke a Word and it came to pass. One of the verses that my pastor, Dr. Rod Parsley, gave us for the year 2023 is Psalm 81:10, which says, *"Open your mouth with a mighty decree, I will fulfill it now, you will see, the words that you speak so shall it be."* (TPT). This prophetic word came as a confirmation because I was already writing this book when we received it.

Let us analyze this verse together. God says, "Open your mouth with a mighty decree," not a weak one, not a negative one, but a powerful declaration. Then He says, "I will fulfill the words that you speak." Words bring life or death. What we speak can create the world we live in. We become the product of what we say about ourselves. Besides the fact that people may say things about us, we also have more power in what we declare. When you look at yourself in the mirror, what do you say? What words come out of your mouth? I meet different people every day, whether it is during my ministry trips, at my home church, or at work. Most of the people I meet always tell me that I inspire them by how confident I am. Well, I was not always like that. This confidence I carry today is the result of God working on me and a journey with the Holy Spirit.

When I was younger, I did not like myself. I kept putting emphasis on the bad parts of my body and the bad parts of my character, until they became my identity. Every morning, I would look at myself in the mirror and say how ugly I was; my nose was big, my eyes were big, there was nothing good there. It was not always people who said those things; I said them to myself. The power of people's opinions about us is contingent on what we believe and say about ourselves.

One day, I met a woman I will never forget in my life. Unfortunately, she has preceded us to be with our heavenly Father; may her soul rest in peace. She was the first woman I opened up to in regards to how I felt about myself. She gave me an exercise and told me to practice it every morning when I woke up, and every night before I went to bed. I want you to do the same thing as you are reading this. She said, "Take a sheet of paper and write all the bad things you think of yourself." She gave me an hour, then said, "I will leave you

46

alone in this room, and I will be back after the set time." For the first ten minutes, my hands were shaking. I had words in my mind; I used to say them every day, but I did not understand why it became so hard for me to write them down.

An article by InnerDrive states that writing down your thoughts and feelings helps you to label your emotions. Labeling is key for understanding what you are feeling and why. This aids your self-awareness as well as your ability to analyze how you think (also known as metacognition). Labeling also helps you to process your feelings, which can reduce the intensity of emotions, enabling you to manage them more effectively.[1] I was in that room, alone. After fighting with my emotions, I was finally able to write everything that I felt. Every word preceded a tear; after every sentence came a few minutes of sobbing. Everything I wrote brought back memories that I did not want to relive again. As I was writing, I saw my younger self, fighting for my little life. I was full of rage, hatred, and bitterness. I wanted to stop every once in a while, but I could feel a hand tapping on my right shoulder. That hour seemed like an eternity until the last punctuation mark. I dropped my pen and felt so empty that no tears were dropping from my eyes.

When she came back, she found me seated with my head on the paper. I cried so much to the point where the paper was almost soaked. She hugged me for a few minutes until I put myself together, and then we sat down. She looked me in the eyes and said, "You have done a great job. It is not everybody

---

[1] InnerDrive

who can face their pain, fear, and emotions the way you just did." Writing is a way of facing your emotions. I was eleven years old; too young to have endured the things I endured. You will understand why as you read. Then she said, "After today, consider all that you wrote on this paper as someone who does not exist." She took the sheet of paper, handed it to me, and asked me to tear it up and put it in a trash bin.

She took another sheet of paper and said, "This is a blank page, and you are given the opportunity to write good things about yourself. You get to create who you want to be and how you want people to identify you." I started writing

"The moment you doubt whether you can fly, you cease forever to be able to do it."—J. M. Barrie

positive words, and it took me longer than it did when I was writing my emotions down. There are more good things about you than bad, so give yourself room to embrace the beauty that you are.

If you struggle with self-confidence, do this same exercise. I am telling you, it is worth it. It is about that time to erase the lies you have been told and those you told yourself. God is ready to fill your mouth with His Word; speak it, declare it, live it.

"There are more good things about you than bad, so give yourself room to embrace the beauty that you are."

#TMAY

Now it's your turn. It's time to face those emotions, and write them down as they come into your mind.

_____

_____

_____

_____

_____

_____

The second exercise that I will have you do is to take sticky notes and write beautiful words of affirmation or Bible verses on them. Stick them near your mirror or on a wall in your bedroom. Every time you pass by them, read them out loud and believe that that is who you are. Here are a few Bible verses that will help you with this exercise:

Have I not commanded you? Be strong and courageous. Do not be afraid; do not be discouraged, for the Lord your God will be with you wherever you go. (Joshua 1:9 – NIV).

For you created my inmost being; you knit me together in my mother's womb. I praise you because I am fearfully and wonderfully made; your works are wonderful, I know that fully well. (Psalm 139:13-14 – NIV).

But those who hope in the Lord will renew their strength. They will soar on wings like eagles; they will run and not grow weary, they will walk and not faint. (Isaiah 40:31 – NIV).

But he said to me, "My grace is sufficient for you, for my power is made perfect in weakness." Therefore I will boast all the more gladly about my weaknesses, so that Christ's power may rest on me. (2 Corinthians 12:9 – NIV).

In fact, even the hairs on your head are all numbered. Do not be afraid; you are more valuable than many sparrows." (Luke 12:7 – NIV).

"You are altogether beautiful, my darling; there is no flaw in you." (Song of Solomon 4:7 – NIV).

"For I know the plans I have for you," declares the Lord, "plans to prosper you and not to harm you, plans to give you hope and a future. Then you will call on me and come and pray to me, and I will listen to you. You will seek me and find me when you seek me with all your heart. I will be found by you," declares the Lord, "and will bring you back from captivity. I will gather you from all the nations and places where I have banished you," declares the Lord, "and will bring you back to the place from which I carried you into exile." (Jeremiah 29:11-14 – NIV).

Now, I want you to declare this after me:

I am blessed and highly favored by God. I was created with a greater purpose to change the world. When God created me on the 6th day, He saw that it was very good. I am beautiful. I am intelligent. I am amazing. I am unique. I am more than enough. I am capable. I am confident. I love myself and God loves me more. I am not a failure. I am not my pain. I am not my trauma. I am who God says I am; a masterpiece, the apple of His eyes. Today, I made a decision to live by the truth of God concerning my life. I speak life over my heart, soul, and spirit. I speak deliverance from every reality that I have created by the words I have spoken in times of pain and trouble. I use my mouth to create good things and dismantle evil ones. As Mark 11:23 says, "Truly I tell you, if anyone says to this mountain, 'Go, throw yourself into the sea,' and does not doubt in their heart but believes that what they say will happen, it will be done for them." I will not only believe with my heart, but I also declare with my mouth.

CHAPTER 6
DEALING WITH INSECURITIES

Now, let's talk about today's real virus called insecurity. By definition, insecurity is a feeling of uncertainty, a lack of confidence, or anxiety about yourself. Most of the time, insecurity is a failure to know one's identity and being confident in it. There are many causes of insecurities, and the major root—the big cause—comes from our childhood. Let me share with you a small portion of my testimony.

I am the youngest of a family of eight; five girls and three boys. A lot of things happened to me while growing up that I had no explanation for. I was always feeling socially distant, and I was always depressed. The only places I went besides being home were school and church.

I grew up catholic, and I remember my parents dragging us to morning masses. Even though I was in an environment with a lot of people and activities, I did not want to be involved in any of it. Besides my biological siblings, we also lived with cousins, nephews and nieces, some uncles and aunts in the same house. My dad was really known for always inviting and hosting people over; sometimes, he wouldn't even think of our safety. It was really a full home, and by that I mean full of different characters to deal with. As a little girl, I saw a lot of toxic patterns happening in my own family; abuse in all types of ways was one of them. Growing up in that kind of environment, I became so distant from anyone because, at some point, I thought people would hurt me. Seeing people fight, sometimes with weapons, made me fear anything and anyone. Just imagine sixteen or more people living together.

My facial expression was always giving signals. I was always angry and unhappy. I felt like I did not know who I was, and there was no reason for me to be alive. Yes, at eight years old, I had suicidal thoughts. I always felt like my siblings were not treating me fairly. Nobody wanted to listen to me, and even when I tried to speak, I would always be interrupted with negative statements and judgment with so much violence. Crying was my way of letting the pain out. I remember sometimes when my sister's friends would come home, they would see me and ask why I was so quiet. My sister would say, "Leave her. She's always like that. She's always that bad." I got so used to hearing bad things about me, for example, "You're good at nothing." All those words started shaping how I viewed myself. I could have considered myself one of the smartest kids at school because I was always among the top five students in my class. I was getting better grades than most of my family members.

Even if I felt proud of myself at school, I would come back home and cry because I was allowing all the bad words to sink into my head. I especially had a father who almost never appreciated anyone's effort. I finished one of my primary school years with 91%, which is really high based on the grading system in my home country, the Democratic Republic of Congo. Nevertheless, I came back home and, guess what my dad told me, "You could have done better." No matter what I did, it was never good enough for others.

When I was ten years old, I started taking Bible lessons at my church with my mentor back then; the one I mentioned earlier. Among the topics we were looking at was one about internal or inner wounds. Since the topic was a little personal, we had some one-on-one sessions weekly with mentors.

One day, we sat outside, and Ms. Pauline started asking me questions. My answers were dry: yes or no. She knew something was wrong, thanks to the gifts of the Holy Spirit. God started revealing certain things to her concerning my life. I started crying. It felt as if someone was rubbing salt in the wounds. That was what I was searching for all those years; someone to help me find the truth about my life and the reasons for my attitudes. After that session, she gave me homework. She told me to go sit with my mom and ask her all the questions I had in mind. Then come back and tell her how it went. When I got home, I told my mom we needed to talk.

Mom was so confused and sad at the same time because she was used to hearing things from me, such as, "I want to know my real father," "Tell me if I was adopted or not," "Bring me to my actual family." I did not feel loved enough, so I concluded that I was not one of them. I mean, who would want to live in that type of environment? I am a strong believer that no family on earth is perfect, but at that age, family drama was the last thing I wanted to deal with. One thing that supported my point was the fact that everyone had pictures of them as babies except me. I was being mocked by my siblings because of that. See, when you are hurt, even the less relevant things trigger you.

Imagine the trauma this little girl was going through. All I needed was answers. I asked my mom why I was going through all those things. She broke down in tears and started telling me about the circumstances under which she got pregnant with me. When she found out that she was pregnant, she announced it to my dad, who did not take it well. He started threatening her to have an abortion to the point where he kicked her out of the house in the middle of the night and told her not to come back until she got rid of the baby. She was so convinced that there was something different about me, and knowing that she had lost a baby years before because of him, she did not want to repeat the same mistake. My mom was spending nights in parking lots. Some family members calmed my dad and brought her back to the house, but it was still insult after insult, abusive language after abusive language, and all that was affecting me even in the womb.

Research shows that emotions can increase particular hormones in a pregnant woman's body, which can affect the baby's developing body and brain.

Let me open a parenthesis here and say, if you are not ready to accept a child in your life as a married couple, find ways not to get pregnant. If, after trying, God still decides to give you a child, learn to love and accept the baby from the day you find out about the pregnancy. If you are not ready to be responsible for someone's life, avoid getting pregnant at all costs. If you still get pregnant or get someone pregnant, wait until the baby is born and give them up for adoption. There are families who cry all day and all night just to get a child.

After my mom told me the story, it all made sense. I understood why I was not feeling loved by my dad. Although physically present, I felt like he was not emotionally present in my life. I grew up feeling like an unwanted child. What I want to focus on here is the fact that I started believing what I was told to be my identity, to the extent where I could look at myself in the mirror and say, "You are not beautiful," "You are good for nothing." All the things I heard about me created insecurities in me.

Years later, I came to understand that my siblings were also dealing with their own insecurities to the point where, intentionally or not, they were just projecting their insecurities on me and on anybody else around. It is called "Psychological Projection." I concluded that they too needed help. This became my prayer burden for God to heal them as well.

Maybe while you are reading this book, the memories of your childhood came to the fore. People made you feel insecure because of your body type, height, weight, the color of your skin, a part of your body, your background, or anything at all.

What is insecurity? According to the Oxford dictionary, insecurity is uncertainty or anxiety about oneself or lack of confidence. An insecure person can easily get frustrated about life because he or she will also use others as a comparison scale. Insecurity causes bitterness in people's hearts. You are insecure if you think that other people's success is your failure or people's progress is your regress. Insecurity causes a lot of issues in relationships. I would also like to add my own definition of insecurity: living a life that is not grounded in Christ. I love the hymn that says, "On Christ the solid rock I stand. All other ground is sinking sand."

Living a life that is not sustained by Christ is setting yourself up for failure and disappointments. The foundation you are building your life on matters. Imagine a man building a house on the sand. The whole house will crumble, right? Well, that is the same thing that happens when you build your confidence, joy, and happiness on your social media followers, on your husband or wife, on your boyfriend or girlfriend, on your family members and friends, on your job, etc., anything but God. Not having a secure foundation will make you insecure.

The Word of God says, *"Therefore everyone who hears these words of mine and puts them into practice is like a wise man who built his house on the rock. The rain came down, the streams rose, and the winds blew and beat against that house; yet it did not fall, because it had its foundation on the rock. But everyone who hears these words of mine and does not put them into practice is like a foolish man who built his house on sand. The rain came down, the streams rose, and the winds blew and beat against that house, and it fell with a great crash." (Matthew 7:24-27 – NIV).* The wind of depression will come, the wind of grief will come, the wind of disappointment will come, the wind of anxiety will come, the wind of people's criticism will come, but because of God's Word inside of you, you will stay standing.

We live in an era where people are insecure and are also surrounded by insecure people.

Insecure people will drag others into their own insecurities, while confident people will uplift others. There are people in life who will happily be your friends because you are more vulnerable than they are, and that is the only way they think their light can shine. There are others who will always try to bring you down and belittle your vision. Baby, shine anyway. Go after that goal anyway. Write that book, open that business, start that podcast, release that song, bring that vision to life. Your circle should inspire you and not despise you. If they do, downgrade the relationship level to followers not friends.

" *Do not allow people to project their insecurities on you. They are responsible for how they feel; you are responsible for how you decide to react to it.* **"**

#TMAY

Paulo Coelho said, *"I am on a diet from bad thoughts, destructive people, and things that are not good for me."* As Christians, we are called to love people, but it does not mean we are supposed to always sit at the same table. That romantic relationship that is making you feel less of a person needs to end now, especially if you are not bound by the institution called marriage. It is time to put an end to that manipulation you call attention and love. You need to leave those rooms where you are not valued enough. Even Jesus, who loves us all, chose twelve people to walk closely with. You need to tell some people, "I love you, but my purpose is calling, and I will need the real 'me' for that, so allow me to go find myself and embrace my identity."

I spent years of my life choosing others but me, pushing people forward while going backward, until Jesus whispered in my ear, *"I came to earth, helped people for thirty-three years, but that did not pause My purpose."* You can push people while pushing yourself too. If it is a win, then we are all in it together. We are all going up, and nobody is left behind, especially not me.

Another root of insecurity is comparison. "He or she got married, so it is time for me to find a partner." "He or she has a baby, but I am here not even dating anyone." "Oh, he or she got a new car. I need to have one too." "X and Y are doing this and are doing that, so I need to be and do the same." See, insecure people use others' standards to adjust their lives. Just because they are ahead of you does not mean you are behind in life. 70% of the close friends I went to school and grew up with are married. 60% of them have kids. Do I sometimes feel sad about not being like them? Yes. Sometimes I think about building a family too, but that does not take away my joy and my peace. While I am waiting, I am still thriving in other areas, living my best life and fulfilling my purpose.

Quit comparing yourself to people out there. Believe me, they alone know what it takes to be who they are and do what you do. They will not always share how unhappy they are with you. All you can see is the tip of the iceberg; there is more to the story. If they live what they share, glory to God. When Jesus multiplied the bread and the fish, the Bible says the baskets were full and everyone ate. Not everyone got access to the basket at the same time, but they all ate and were satisfied (see Matthew 14).

I always consider life as the traffic signals in a four-way intersection. People on the red lights have to stop; those on the green light are allowed to proceed. It does not matter how long the people at the red light wait, they will also be given a signal to move. If all cars try to proceed at the same time, there will be chaos. Wait for your turn, but do not grow bitter while waiting. There are a lot more aspects of life to enjoy than what you do not have. In due time, God will surely make it happen.

Today, I want you to remove all those lies and take the truth of the Word of God that says, "I am fearfully and wonderfully made" (see Psalm 139:14). You are God's wonder, and everything about you is perfect. After I went through a healing process, I entered a season that I call "detox," meaning I started getting rid of all the unhealthy meanings I had given to my life and all the bad words I myself have spoken or others had said to me. I got rid of the views I had of myself and the perception people had of me, and I adopted God's language. I learned to see myself through God's eyes and be content with the person He allows me to be every day.

Decide to change your language now. The Bible tells the story of Naomi who, after losing her husband and sons, went back to Moab. At the entrance of the city, people started asking, "Can this be Naomi?" She replied, "Don't call me Naomi, call me Mara" (see Ruth 1:20). The name Naomi means "pleasantness" but because of the situations she encountered, Naomi changed her identity. She adapted her language to what she had been through. Let me tell you this, you are not, and you will never be, the problem you are facing in life. You are not your trauma; not even the abuse you went through. None of those things can define who you are. Decide today to declare good things about yourself.

I would like you to say this prayer with me:

> "Lord, I will not let the world define who I am or distort what You have said about me. I may have had a traumatic childhood. I may have gone through divorce. I may have lost a family member. I may have gone through depression. I may have gone through a breakup, but I believe that Your plans for me are good, and I believe my pain will serve purpose. I pray that You heal my heart from bitterness. I pray that You deliver me from self-sabotage. As of today, Your Word will be in my mouth, in Jesus' name. Amen.

" When Jesus multiplied the bread and the fish, the Bible says the baskets were full, and everyone could eat. Not everyone got access to the basket at the same time, but they all ate and were satisfied. "

#TMAY

Write aspects of your life where you feel insecure. After that, ask God to heal you and replace those lies with His truth.

CHAPTER 7
COMPROMISE

One of the biggest viruses attacking this generation, especially the church, is compromise. It looks less important until we see the real chaos it brings to people's lives and to our society.

What is compromise? According to the Cambridge dictionary, compromise is to accept that you will reduce your demands or change your opinion in order to reach an agreement with someone. In other words, lowering your standards to agree with something or someone. Well, compromise is not always a bad thing; a new mom might lose some hours of sleep taking care of her newborn; however, to what extent are we willing to compromise? We all have principles we live by that shape our personality. The ability to know which ones are negotiable and which ones are not is very crucial.

One of the problems with today's generation is that we are ready to give up on values, morals, and principles, and we are ready to lower our expectations to fit in society. It is sad to even see how low Christians today will go to fit in with what this new world calls the "norm." My spiritual father, Dr. Pastor Rod Parsley, always says, *"As Christians, we are not abnormal in a normal world, we are normal in an abnormal world."* The thought of considering that we are not fit because we stand on our Christian principles lead many to compromise their faith. Let's go to the Bible and read the story of a man called Daniel.

In Daniel 1, the Jews were held captives by Babylon. King Nebuchadnezzar commanded the officials to bring some of them so they could be trained in the Babylonian way. Daniel 1:3 says, *"Then the king ordered Ashpenaz, chief of his court officials, to bring into the king's service some of the Israelites from the royal family and the nobility."* (NIV). Notice that the king was looking for people from the royal families. The enemy knows who you are, and he knows your worth, sometimes even more than you. Even when he attacks, he does not just go after anybody. The enemy attacks royalty. He often attacks people who have something valuable inside of them. If you are under attack by the enemy or if you ever become a target to the devil, it is because he knows your value.

The devil is always after the areas and the people whom God has His eyes on. Daniel 1:4 says, *"Young men without any*

" *As Christians, we are not abnormal in a normal world, we are normal in an abnormal world.* **"**
— *Dr. Rod Parsley*

#TMAY

physical defect, handsome, showing aptitude for every kind of learning, well informed, quick to understand, and qualified to serve in the king's palace." (NIV). King Nebuchadnezzar wanted to teach them the language and literature of the Babylonians. The king was very specific in his request; so is the devil when he wants to destroy a generation. He asked for young men without any physical defect, handsome, showing aptitude for every kind of learning, well-informed, quick to understand, and qualified to serve in the king's palace. We can see here that the enemy's target is the youth. The devil is after our children and their innocence, after our brothers and sisters.

The king wanted to teach them when they were young the ways out of God's will. This is what we are experiencing today. What are they teaching our children in schools? Toddlers are now growing up confused because they are told that there are more than two genders. What in the world is happening, church?

We are living under a Babylonian influence that is trying to get us outside of the will of God and our identity in Christ. The king separated the young men from their families, and this is what the devil is doing in families right now. Children are getting out of control; teenager's attitudes are getting out of hand. It is time for parents to spend more time with their children, training them according to the Word of God. The Bible says in Proverbs 22:6, *"Train up a child in the way he should go; even when he is old he will not depart from it."* (NIV).

The Jews knew the God of their fathers. Those young men knew the law of God, but they were brought to Babylon and were taught about other gods whom they had to worship. Our kids are learning about Jesus in our homes, but once they are exposed to the outside world—school, social media, clubs, and so on—they are presented with other gods; idols such as drugs, alcohol, porn, sex, crime, etc. The devil is taking God's people, teaching them magic, voodoo, spell casting, and how to pray with candles and cards. We see sexual immorality, etc., on TikTok these days, so our children are getting off track with God. The devil is not after evil; he is after what is good so he can influence and destroy. I pray, in the name of Jesus Christ, that our children are coming back to God. Our youth will be set on fire for God again. I cancel the devil's calendar for this generation. Every soul, mind, body, and spirit are being loose now. I pray that God gives parents the strength to nurture their children according to His will. May the altar of prayer burn again in our homes. May God raise a generation that will say no to the Babylonian system and impose the kingdom of God. I pray that our government will not just use the Bible to take an oath but will use the Word of God to rule with.

The story continues. Among those men taken to Babylon was Daniel. Daniel 1:8 says that Daniel resolved not to defile himself with the royal food and wine and asked the chief official for permission not to defile himself this way. There are two things I want to mention here. First, Daniel resolved not to eat the king's food, meaning it was a personal decision coming from an understanding of his identity. He was bold enough to stand up for himself. One may ask, what was wrong with the food? Jewish law forbids the eating of meat that is sacrificed to idols. The great King Nebuchadnezzar and his kingdom worshiped other gods and made sacrifices to them. Eating the same food sacrificed to idols would imply worshiping those idols as well. It is time for Christians today to know where to draw the line. It is time to put some boundaries on your exposure. What food are you eating? With what do you feed your heart, mind, and spirit? Just because it looks good does not mean it is good for YOU. Your spirit cannot afford every diet. What food does your social media serve you? What food do your friends and family serve you? Let me even shock some of you; What food does your church serve you?

Ezekiel 3:3 says, "Son of man eat the scroll I am giving you and fill your stomach with it." God gave Ezekiel His Word before He sent him to speak to His people. If whatever food is served to you does not come from the Word of God, whether it is the church, government or world in general that serves it, you should not eat and take part in it.

Nowadays, the line between the church and the world is getting thinner because we have a church with no boundaries. We have church in the world, and the world in the church.

Secondly, Daniel asked for permission from the chief officials not to eat the food for ten days. Daniel not only stood for his faith and principles but also showed respect to the officials. It is possible to stand your ground without disrespecting the authorities. It is possible to refuse to compromise in a polite way, with such wisdom as Daniel.

" *I pray that our government will not just use the Bible to take an oath, but will use the Word of God to rule with.* **"**

#TMAY

This story from the book of Daniel is a reflection of the era we now live in. Some Christians today would never put their lives on the line to not conform to the Babylonian way of life. The Bible says in Romans 12:2, *"Do not conform to the patterns of this world but be transformed by the renewing of your mind." (NIV).* Christians today are blending in with the society; living like everyone else, speaking like everyone else, and behaving like everyone else. We are not from this world, Beloved. Our identity is not found in this world. We are children of God. We belong to His kingdom; therefore, we should have the kingdom culture and not the world culture.

We identify ourselves according to heaven's criteria, not the world. Daniel and his three friends were not the only young men who were taken captives. The rest could not resist the pressure and were easily influenced. Some Christians do the same thing every time they find themselves in a non-Christian territory or environment, whether it is at school, work, or just hanging out with non-Christian friends. Jesus hung out with sinners, sat at the table with some of them, got His feet washed by one, but never became like them. In fact, He influenced them to become like Him. We are called to love sinners but not love sin. There is a big difference right there.

The captives were given several opportunities—including free education and training—but at the cost of losing their identity and faith. Mind you, even their names had to be changed. Your name is a symbol of identity. The other captives may have said to themselves, "What an exciting opportunity! We are slaves, but now we have a chance to level up." Is expressing our faith in the one true God worth ruining such a future? You can be a king with the devil but still be a slave. The Hebrew boys could have said, "Why risk our lives when a little compromise would put an end to so many problems and so much stress? Why force things?" When things are going well, why would you go against it?

This world will also give us opportunities. The devil will bait us with things that we like; material things, per se, for example, money, houses, cars, fame, etc., but nothing is worth compromising your faith. Nothing is worth forfeiting your soul. Matthew 16:26-27 says, *"and what do you benefit if you gain the whole world but lose your own soul? Is anything worth more than your soul? For the Son of Man will come with His angels in the glory of His Father to judge all people according to their deeds." (NLT).*

I grew up in a Christian environment with people who spend more time in church buildings and share a Christian faith. I got involved in church activities at a young age. Therefore, there are things I could not do because of my faith and the type of education I grew up with. My father was a very religious man who was involved in lots of church activities. He cared about his image, so as his children, we had to watch after ourselves. I could not behave in certain ways. I could not go to certain places or hang out with certain people. Even when I started dating in my teenage era, I did not lower the bar for some boundaries I had set. There are things that I couldn't allow myself to do compared to most of my friends.

In July 2016, I came to the United States of America. Like Daniel, who was brought to Babylon, things were way different for me. I had friends who were accustomed to clubbing, drinking alcohol, sleeping with men, listening to worldly music, and all the things you may think of.

I even remember some of my friends back in Africa telling me that once I stepped on American soil, I would give up on God. I was happy to disappoint them. I was living in such a hostile environment where I was being mocked for not living like them. Was it easy? No. Did I lose friends? Yes. I was depicted as the bad girl who thought being Christian made her a better person. The first two years in this new culture were a season of trials for me. However, like the Bible says, *'Not by might nor by power, but by My Spirit,' Says the Lord of hosts. (Zechariah 4:6 - NKJV).* God gave me the strength I needed. I knew who I was; my identity became my force. Am I perfect? No. Did I fall in some areas? Yes. But God would remind me of who I am and His Word every time, and I would quickly get back to my senses.

I recently watched a movie titled "I am not ashamed." The movie was so inspiring that after I watched it, I ran to my computer to include it in this book. It is a movie based on the real story of a seventeen-year-old, Rachel Joy Scott, a student at Columbine High School in the late 90s. Rachel was a young teenager who was not afraid to speak of her faith, even at the cost of losing her friends. Despite the rejection from the people around her and the betrayal of her close friend who cheated with her boyfriend, Rachel did not give up on her faith. Instead, she kept on forgiving and praying for them. Rachel became an inspiration to many around her. Below is one of her statements found in her diaries:

"I have no more personal friends at school, but you know what? I am not going to apologize for speaking the name of Jesus. I am not going to justify my faith to them, and I am not going to hide the light that God has put in me. If I have to sacrifice everything, I will. I will take it. If my friends have to become my enemies for me to be with my best friend, Jesus, then that's fine with me."

On April 20th, 1999, Rachel was shot on campus. She was among thirteen who were killed. However, even when the shooter asked her, after shooting her twice in the leg and once in the back, if she still believed in God, Rachel's response did not change. Today, Rachel's story has changed many people's lives, starting with the same friends who mocked her faith. One of the words she left in her diary states, "I have this theory that if one person can go out of their way to show compassion, then it will start a chain reaction of the same. People will never know how far a little kindness can go."

As Christians, we are called to be different, set apart for God, and to reflect the nature of God. The Bible says creation is eagerly waiting for the manifestation of the sons of God (see Romans 8:19). We must stand in faith.

One of the tools the devil is using to make Christians compromise is social media. People are being led by trends and challenges that they see on the internet.

It is hard to know the difference between Christians and non-Christians as they all carry Bibles and post scriptures, yet live unholy. The same Instagram account that says "preacher" is the same account that defends homosexuality. The same account that speaks of God creating all life and sustains it is the same account speaking in favor of abortion.

It is time to get your identity back. It is time for the true gospel to be preached. Compromise has not only affected regular believers but is now affecting church leadership. Pastors can no longer preach on sanctification because they fear offending their congregation. Ministers can no longer speak the truth because they are afraid of losing followers on social media. Prophets can no longer be led by "Thus saith the Lord" because they are afraid of the government. We are born again to make a difference; we are to reflect God in everything we say and do. We need to be distinct from the culture.

Daniel and his friends, while in Babylon, did not refuse to learn the language and literature of the Babylonians. What they refused was to eat at the king's table as the food was sacrificed to idols. This is a perfect example that we can still take advantage of the opportunities given in this world, such as getting our education, becoming successful and having a big platform of influence, becoming entrepreneurs, renowned artists, and book writers without actually compromising our faith. For us Christians, to reach as many souls as we need to for Christ, to manifest the power of God in this world, we also need those different platforms. I personally do not encourage preachers who do not motivate the people in their congregations to go to school, get degrees, and have a life besides ministry and beyond the four walls of the church. Our true Christianity is not manifested in the church or among our

Christian fellows but outside the church, in the world. The Bible says, *"You are the light of the world. A city that is set on a hill cannot be hidden. Nor do they light a lamp and put it under a basket, but on a lampstand, and it gives light to all who are in the house." (Matthew 5:14-15 – NKJV).* Light shines in the darkness; we are called to influence the world.

What are the areas where you feel that you compromise your faith the most? List them and ask the Holy Spirit to give you strength.

(Finding the real "you" will require facing the vulnerable "you.")

_____

_____

_____

_____

_____

_____

_____

_____

_____

_____

_____

_____

_____

CHAPTER 8
GET TO KNOW HIM

S ince creation, God's desire was always to be closer to men and have a relationship with them. He created man and woman so He can find partners and friends in them. Genesis 3:8 says, *"And they heard the sound of the Lord walking in the garden in the cool of the day, and Adam and his wife hid themselves from the presence of the Lord God among the trees of the garden." (NKJV).*

God walking in the garden implies closeness and intimacy; it means that beside Him being God, He wants to relate as much as He can to humans. God was in the habit of walking in the garden to have fellowship with Adam and Eve until sin entered. For centuries, humanity has lost that closeness to God to the point where God established specific people, such as prophets, priests, etc. to become mediators between Him and men. Thank God, Jesus came to earth, died on the cross, and came back to life after three days to restore that relationship with God, the intimacy we once lost.

God wants to get closer to you today. He wants to reveal Himself to you. He wants you to know Him. God loves us so much that He gives us ways to connect with Him. Getting to know who you are is through getting to know who He is. You might be asking yourself, "How do I get to know God?" I will give you three ways to do so.

First, you need to manifest the desire to know Him. Philippians 3:10 says, *"[For my determined purpose is] that I may know Him [that I may progressively become more deeply and intimately acquainted with Him, perceiving and recognizing and understanding the wonders of His Person more strongly and more clearly], and that I may in that same way come to know the power outflowing from His resurrection [which it exerts over believers], and that I may so share His sufferings as to be continually transformed [in spirit into His likeness even] to His death, [in the hope]." (AMPC).* You need to desire Him, and the more you do, the more He reveals Himself to you, and the more you get to know yourself.

Secondly, dedicate more time to Him. Just imagine two people, male and female, who fall in love with each other and start dating. At the beginning of the relationship, you will notice that they would spend more time together. They will not allow a few minutes or hours to pass without checking on each other, either via call or text. Some even spend the night on a Facetime call throughout the night, even falling asleep until one of them wakes up to end the call. We have all been there, right? There is this constant desire to spend time together, and actually spending time either virtually or in person will help strengthen the relationship and help them get to know each other more deeply. As time goes by, they start to become familiar with each other's behavior and language, even the nonverbal ones.

Have you ever noticed a woman who has been moody all day, then when her husband comes, he says, "She needs food." As soon as she eats, she becomes happier. This means they have spent so much time together that they can read through each other's silence.

This applies to our relationship with God as well. Spend more time with Him to get to know Him, how He speaks and how He operates. One of the most important keys to any relationship is love. When you love someone, you want to spend more time with the person. There is no one busier than someone who doesn't love you. They will hang up on a call just to close the fridge. They will find all the reasons in the world not to spend time with you. A person who loves you, no matter how busy they are, will find time in their agenda for you.

Imagine how busy God is, yet He came in human form to spend thirty-three years physically with men, then gave us His Spirit, who is forever with us. It is all about priority. Is God a priority in your life? How important is it for you to know Him? The answers to these questions will determine how well you will get to know Him. You need to be intentional about the time you want to spend with Him.

We learn more about God and spend time with Him through prayer. Prayer is a dialogue with God. It is telling Him what is on your mind, and also listening to what is in His heart. Many Christians have a one-way relationship with God. They pray when they need something from God, but after they are done with their requests, the prayer is over. This approach will never get you closer to Him. The Bible says that John, the disciple of Jesus, whom He loved the most, was leaning on His chest (see John 13:23). This was not just a physical position, but it was also a spiritual one. By leaning on someone's chest, you can feel their heartbeat; you will know how fast or how slow it beats. It gave John a sensation of closeness to Jesus.

Prayer is a two-way street. Let Him hear you, and you listen to Him. Prayer is essential to build a solid relationship with God. The Bible says that Jesus, very early in the morning while it was still dark, got up, left the house and went off to a solitary place where He prayed (see Mark 1:35). If Jesus, the Son of God, prayed, so should we.

The third way to spend time with God is through His Word. You need to read your Bible daily. Joshua 1:8 says, *"This Book of the Law shall not depart from your mouth, but you shall meditate in it day and night, that you may observe to do according to all that is written in it. For then you will make your way prosperous, and then you will have good success."* *(NKJV)*. Reading the Word does not only help you know Him better, but it also helps you know you better. Remember, we were created in His image, meaning, as He is, so are we (see 1 John 4:17). The Word of God is like you looking in a mirror when you wake up, seeing the reflection of yourself, facing the real you, no filter, no makeup, just you. Mediating on the Word of God is not just reading it but reflecting on and applying it to your daily life.

The devil understands the importance of knowing the Word of God. That is why he plays with your ignorance to make you believe in who you are not. The Bible says we perish for lack of knowledge (see Hosea 4:6). You want to know where the confusion we have in this current world comes from? Lack of knowledge. The less we know the truth, the easier it will be for us to believe in the lie. The more we know the truth, the harder it will be for us to believe in the lie.

The less we know the truth, the easier it will be for us to believe in the lie. The more we know the truth, the harder it will be for us to believe in the lie.

People are spending more time in front of their screens, reading newspapers, letting the news penetrate their mind, body, and soul, and still asking why the world is upside down? The truth is, we have gone far from the truth of God and have made lies our reality. The world is living in fear because we really don't have the knowledge of the Word of God; therefore, we do not know Him.

It is time for us to get back to spending more time with God. Create time in your calendar to spend time with your Lord and Savior. Sometimes you will not even have to speak; just be there in His presence and listen. What changed my life at the age of twelve was not the words that came from my mouth, it was His presence that penetrated me and started doing the work inside. Let Him start the work inside of you. It will not always be pretty; the process might be ugly at times, but just surrender, it is worth it. I am not asking you to spend hours in prayer. Every journey starts with one step. You can start by dedicating thirty minutes a day with God, whether in the morning, afternoon or evening. Follow this for two weeks, then go for one hour a day, and so on. I am telling you, your life will never be the same. Be consistent in your prayer life.

Write a time for each day of the week below where you want to have a one-on-one with God.

Monday _____

Tuesday _____

Wednesday _____

Thursday _____

Friday _____

Saturday _____

Sunday _____

CHAPTER 9
IT'S IN THE WORD

T he more you know about yourself, the more you become conscious of the power you have over the enemy. Identity in Christ is not just about knowing the Word of God but understanding how we relate to it and how to use it. The devil knows the Word of God too; the proof is in Matthew 4:1-4, *"Then Jesus was led up by the Spirit into the wilderness to be tempted by the devil. And when He had fasted forty days and forty nights, afterward He was hungry. Now when the tempter came to Him, he said, "If You are the Son of God, command that these stones become bread." But He answered and said, "It is written, 'Man shall not live by bread alone, but by every word that proceeds from the mouth of God.'" (NKJV).* Just like Jesus, we are also tempted by the devil in many ways and, most of the time, he comes whispering and making us doubt the validity of the Word of God. How did Jesus react? Jesus rebuked him with the same word, but the difference is that Jesus had more power because He knew who He was and also understood that His identity was connected to the Word.

So many people know the Word of God but ignore its effect on their lives. Scripture becomes just memorized words and phrases. Your identity comes from the Word of God, and that is your power to defeat the enemy. The Bible says God's people perish for lack of knowledge (see Hosea 4:6). The devil will do his best to keep you away from the truth of the Word of God and make you stay stuck in believing his lies. The devil and his demons can tell who is who. They can catch our spiritual stature. He knows how to differentiate people who know who they are in Christ and people who don't. In Acts 19:13-15, the Bible speaks of the sons of Sceva. *"Then some of the itinerant Jewish exorcists took it upon themselves to call the name of the Lord Jesus over those who had evil spirits, saying, "We exorcise you by the Jesus whom Paul preaches." Also there were seven sons of Sceva, a Jewish chief priest, who did so. And the evil spirit answered and said, "Jesus I know, and Paul I know; but who are you?""" (NKJV).* They used the Word of God; they used the name of Jesus but still had no power over demons.

If you don't know your identity in God, it will make you vulnerable in the eyes of the enemy. The problem is, we have people who have memorized verses, and memorized Christian songs but are not conscious enough of what they say. It is okay to know the Word but add to that; knowing one's identity is way better. Just imagine a president of the country who is getting ready to deliver a speech about a new bill. The speechwriter would make sure the speech is ready before the event. He might go over what he wrote repeatedly. He might even read it to someone else just to make sure it is perfect. However, when the president reads that speech, the impact will be different from when the speechwriter reads it. Why? The president's identity and authority bring more power to that speech. Understand and embrace the fact that you are a child of God, and just knowing that will bring power to everything you declare.

The world will have you look for your identity in external things, such as your career, education, finances, marital and social status, power, success, etc. but none of these are solid foundations to build your identity on. There is more to us than just what we do and own in life. You might have a job today and lose it tomorrow. You might fail in one career path and choose another. You might experience a financial loss; you might experience a divorce. If we depend on these factors to determine who we are, we might as well be confused, lost, and disappointed at some point. Nevertheless, the Word of God is unchanging; it is a strong foundation.

As I explained in my introduction, the Word of God is the manual God sent us to earth with. You cannot use an Apple manual to understand how an Android works or vice versa. In the same way, you cannot use the world's standards to understand who you are. The Bible says we are in the world but we are not of the world (see John 17:14). We do not belong

91

here. We have our heavenly citizenship in the kingdom of God, and we live by its rules.

Jesus says in John 17:14-16, *"I have given them Your word; and the world has hated them because they are not of the world, just as I am not of the world. I do not pray that You should take them out of the world, but that You should keep them from the evil one. They are not of the world, just as I am not of the world."* God gave us His Word to help us in the short journey we call life on earth.

In John 4, the Bible tells the story of Jesus who met a Samaritan woman at a well. The woman had a bad reputation and was known for already having five husbands and was living with one who was not her husband. That was the identity she carried in the world. That was how people saw her and how she saw herself. But the day she met Jesus, the Word made flesh (see John 1:14), her identity changed. She went from adulterer to evangelist. She was introduced to her identity in Christ because of one encounter with the Word of God made flesh, Jesus.

Take time to meditate on the Word until it becomes your life. Read the Word to know God, and read it to know you. As Jesus saw the Woman at the Well's past; her sinful life and mistakes, God sees you the same way because you are not always what you go through when it comes to God. Learn to use the authority that is in the Word of God. Speak it every morning and every night because when the Word of God is spoken by a man or woman who knows their identity, it becomes a weapon and a shield. Be reminded every day that you are who your Father in heaven says you are, not the world, not your circumstances, but Him and Him alone.

Pray this prayer with me:

> Heavenly Father, I decide today to build my identity on Your Word. I understand that my identity is not defined by what I do for a living or by how the world sees me but by how You define me in Your Word. Holy Spirit, reveal Yourself to me and help me find myself in the Word. I disconnect myself from the lies of the devil pertaining to my identity, and I take the Word of God as my every day truth, in Jesus' name. Amen.

CHAPTER 10
YOUR PURPOSE IS ATTACHED TO IT

Identity is understanding who we are. Purpose is understanding the role we play in society. So, we can deduce that identity and purpose are related but one comes before the other. Knowing your identity will help you evolve as a person. By discovering your identity, you give yourself room to change, improve, and make adjustments. Moreover, your identity will help you narrow and discern your passions in life, your goals, and your purpose.

When I was a kid, I decided that I really wanted to be a journalist. Two years later, I made up my mind to become a fashion designer instead. I kept going back and forth from one career goal to another to the point where I just wanted to be and do everything. As I grew up, I began to understand that life is not as simple as I thought. Life is made up of choices, and specific ones. I started my identity discovery process when I turned twelve, and that was when I also started having personal encounters with God.

One thing about me, I love music. I don't think I will ever detach myself from it. My mother used to sing in the senior adult choir, and she would take me with her to rehearsals every week until I started singing with them. Imagine a little girl singing with people from the early 40s to late 80s. I didn't complain because I enjoyed it and I was talented. When I turned eight, my mom made me join the youth choir. Still, I was one of the two youngest members. At least I felt comfortable enough there. From that time until I turned twelve, singing was just expressing a gift to me. I thought I was there just because I could sing. I thought I was there just to fill a seat, but there was more. At twelve, I remember sitting on my bed, and questioning God about a lot of things that I had to endure.

If you read the previous chapters, I gave you a glimpse of my childhood experience. In that conversation, God told me, "There is a purpose for your voice. Your voice is not just a talent, it is a weapon that I will use to impact lives and spread the Gospel." By that, He meant my voice in singing and my voice in speaking. He told me to take my Bible and put it on my chest. Once I did that, I felt like somebody was feeding me with papers. I saw Bible verses passing in front of my eyes. I started weeping and fell to the floor. It took me hours to get back up. I then understood what happened to Ezekiel in the

Bible. Ezekiel 3:1-3, *"Moreover He said to me, "Son of man, eat what you find; eat this scroll, and go, speak to the house of Israel." So I opened my mouth, and He caused me to eat that scroll. And He said to me, "Son of man, feed your belly, and fill your stomach with this scroll that I give you." So I ate, and it was in my mouth like honey in sweetness."* God fed me with His Word so I knew who I was and what I was called to be. Since then, my life has never been the same. From that conversation with God, I knew who I was. I was no longer singing just because I could; I started singing knowing that someone's life depended on my worship. That was when I stopped singing and started serving. There is a big difference between the two. Singing only is a gift showcase; singing while serving is ministry. That marked the beginning of my journey with God and my ministry.

Understand that it will be hard for you to live your purpose if you don't understand your identity first. Thinking that you are just anyone will make you take just any decision. Not knowing who you are is like being in a room with no assigned seat. Not knowing who you are is like wearing a shoe two sizes bigger or smaller than what you should wear. That is where a lot of frustrations we experience in life come from. That conversation with God helped me know what path to follow to become who He intended me to be and what He created me for. Life became way easier for me.

You are probably in the same position I was in. You are not sure of who you are or why you are on earth. You don't know what to do with your life or you doubt that the path you chose is the right one. You really don't know what motivates you,

" Singing only is a gift showcase; singing while serving is ministry. That marked the beginning of my journey with God and my ministry. **"**

#TMAY

and you feel stuck in certain areas of your life. You may have been in this process of finding yourself for years or decades. Whatever the case, it is not too late to find out about who you are. Jeremiah 29:11 says, *"I know the plans that I have for you..."* God knows everything about you. He is the Architect of your life. He sent you to earth with a purpose. Let God help you find "you." Let Him order your steps. Let the Holy Spirit take the wheel of your life. The Psalmist David says, *"The Lord is my shepherd, I shall not lack. He makes me lie down in green pastures, He leads me besides still waters." (Psalm 23:1-2 – NKJV).* Sheep always trust the shepherd because he knows where green pastures are, and because He cares for them. God is your Shepherd. He knows what is good for you; the career, marriage, relationships, etc.

Knowing your identity is crucial if you want to live the life you love. It helps you not only live better but also make the world around you a better place. Embracing your identity is important because it gives you more confidence in the choices you make in life; where you should be, with whom you should be, and what you should do. This is why I strongly encourage single people to make sure they know themselves fully before they make the choice to commit to marrying someone else. If you don't know yourself, on what grounds will you choose your spouse? If you don't know your purpose, how will you know that the man or woman you are choosing will help you fulfill it? Marriage is not just a legal institution; marriage is a covenant where two people decide to come together and fulfill the purpose of God on earth.

Also, not using the Word of God to discover your identity will make you make decisions outside God's will. If you find your identity in the world, you might as well fall into the confusion it comes with. School will not teach you who you are; your friends won't either. You can only find your real identity in God, through His Word. Just imagine yourself playing a puzzle. Before you even start putting pieces together, you need to know the big picture you are trying to create. This applies to life as well. Knowing your identity and your purpose will help you discern who and what fits into your life or not.

I pray that God helps you live in your purpose. May He give you the gift of discernment to know what paths to take. May He help you be in the rooms you are to be and surrounded by the people He Himself will find fit for the type of purpose that is on your life.

I pray for all single people reading this. Marriage is the most important decision after giving your life to Christ. A bad marriage will have you walk out of God's calling. Marrying a man or woman who is not meant for you and with whom you are not equally yoked will make you walk away from God's will. If you know that there is a big purpose and calling on your life, do not take that decision lightly.

A wrong marriage can be a cemetery for your ministry. May God help you find yourself, then assist you in your choices.

" *Always remember that marrying a man or woman who does not bring fire to your anointing will turn your oil into grease, and that is where the flow will stop.* **"**

#TMAY

Write down what you believe are your goals, purpose, and visions, and ask God to either approve them or re-adjust them according to His will (ref: Proverbs 19:21).

CHAPTER 11
FILTERS

W e currently live in an era called "the Information Age," also known as the Computer, New Media or Digital Age. With this technological evolution also came social media. This has helped us connect with each other and share our thoughts, emotions, experiences, etc. This has become a vital part of today's society. There are a lot of benefits that individuals and businesses have gained from this technological evolution. For example, individuals stay in touch with each other through videos and audio calls, messages, pictures, and so on, and businesses reach more customers by their visibility on different platforms.

Nevertheless, when social media is misused, it leads to more harm than good. One of the features that social media apps offer is "filters." With this feature, people can take pictures and videos with smaller noses, bigger lips, smooth skin, etc. Some of them even add makeup to natural faces. I believe that the purpose of these features was just entertainment; however, this is bringing this generation far more than expected. The filter trend has triggered people's insecurities to the point where they want it to become their reality by getting surgeries and body transformation, at least, for those who can afford it. As for those who cannot, bitterness has become their cup of tea.

Whatever people post on social media is not always the true story about their lives. We all choose what to post and, most of the time, we always post ourselves when we look the best. A couple will post a picture of themselves living happily ever after while dealing with divorce behind closed doors. Someone might post a picture with luxury cars and mansions that are photoshopped in; it does not belong to them. It is sad that people don't only use filters on their faces, but they use filters on their lives, giving people an image and showing a personality they do not have. Consequently, a lot of people, especially the youth, are dealing with identity crises and confusion because they think that this is where they find their essence from. That is a pure lie, and if you are one of those, this book is dedicated to you.

> *We need to be aware that filters are not reality and reels are not real.*

We have a generation of so-called influencers who are, unfortunately, deceiving teenagers and young adults and destroying their morals and values. People's mental health is being affected. Some are drowning in depression because they feel less than their peers; others are committing suicide because they feel they are not accepted, and all this for a virtual lie.

The devil has been using social media as a weapon because he knows that: **whatever reaches your eyes and ears have access to your heart, and whatever has access to your heart can dictate your life.**

The Bible says, *"Guard your heart with all diligence, for from it flow springs of life." (Proverbs 4:23 – Berean Standard Bible).* Guarding your heart means paying attention to what you allow yourself to believe and live by because from it flows your thoughts and actions. It means filtering what has access to your soul, mind, and spirit.

People are seeing celebrities all over the world as their role models. Just because you have at least ten thousand followers and a blue check—which you pay for monthly by the way and it is not even earned as it used to be—you now think others should learn something from you. Jesus Christ is our role model. He wanted to relate to humanity so badly that He, who is God, has become flesh, born from a woman, grew up and lived on earth, and faced the same realities we are facing to show us that it is possible to be in a foreign world yet not compromise ourselves. It is possible to be human and godly.

" Whatever reaches your eyes and ears have access to your heart, and whatever has access to your heart can dictate your life. **"**

#TMAY

It is possible to live in the world and by the Word. It is possible to embrace one's identity in God and live a life full of purpose.

1 Peter 2:21 says, *"For this you have been called, because Christ also suffered for you, leaving an example, so that you might follow his steps." (ESV).* It is time for you to get your confidence back. Do not let filtered lives on social media deceive you. You are called for so much greater than that.

We think social media is free and is only there to entertain us; however, when we do not have control over it, social media costs lives and destinies. It harms people's physical, spiritual, and mental health and contributes to a poor body image. Here are some statistics concerning the link between social media and mental health: The National Institute of Mental Health reports that the lifetime prevalence of any mental health illness among adolescents is 49.5%, and 22.2% of adolescents will suffer from a severe mental impairment in their lifetimes. More than 6 out of 10 men and 5 out of 10 women have a social media addiction. Social media has affected a lot of people's intimacy with God. People are trading their prayer life for reels.

We are filling our minds with junk information that is leading us to live a life that is out of the will of God. It takes a lot of discipline to know how to be on those platforms and have a right mind. I do not know if other non-apple phones have the same feature, but with my iPhone, I am able to see my screen time with precision on how much time I spend on apps. The day I discovered that feature, I was in shock. I used to spend almost twelve hours per day on social media. You might say,

"But you use social media for ministry," but at that time, I was not really posting a lot of ministry content. So, basically, those hours were me scrolling through posts, reels, stories, and watching lives. I also realized that my prayer life changed suddenly. I was not dedicating much time to God as I used to do. Moreover, I experienced depression in the same period because I was feeding my mind with a lot of unnecessary things. For example, I was watching videos of people getting proposed to, getting married, posts of pregnancy reveals, and baby showers, so I started questioning where I was at in life. I started doubting the promises of God in my life. It was not that I was single with no man in my DMs because men were still approaching me. I had solicitations almost every week, but I knew who I was and what type of man I needed. So, none of them matched the type of destiny I have.

Seeing all those contents every day almost made me compromise and forget my identity. I told myself I would choose any man among those who are showing their interest in me, forgetting that marrying the majority of them would put an end to my ministry. But because I was feeling pressured, I almost made that mistake. Again, the Holy Spirit reproached me and told me to reduce my screen time and increase my prayer time. He may be saying the same thing to you. Once I did that, I could feel my mind being renewed, and the depression left. This experience made me conclude that social media is a good tool if we know how to use it.

In Philippians 4:8, Paul says, *"And now, dear brothers and sisters, one final thing. Fix your thoughts on what is true, and honorable, and right, and pure, and lovely, and admirable.*

Think about things that are excellent and worthy of praise." *(NLT).* It is time to unfollow some accounts whose contents do not edify you; it is time to put boundaries on what can access your heart.

It is time to get your mind and confidence back. Social media is a virtual world where people post what they think the world will like, but life is more important because it is real.

CHAPTER 12
LABELS

Growing up with a black mom resulted in me having trust issues when it comes to product labels. People who spend time with me know that I am a forever ice cream lover. I always joke around and say if my doctor ever prohibits me from eating ice cream, I will find another doctor. That is how badly I enjoy it. Every day, after school, I would go home, take off my shoes, throw my backpack on the bed and run to the kitchen. First thing first, I would open the fridge and find something to eat. One day, I got home, did my routine, opened the fridge and saw a bowl of ice cream. How did I know it was ice cream? It had a label on it, "French Vanilla Ice Cream," which was literally my favorite. I know what you just thought, "Too basic." Yes, I have heard that all my life, and no one has ever changed my mind about it.

Anyway, I opened the bowl with so much excitement, until I realized that the container was full of frozen vegetables. My heart sank. I was so disappointed, and I couldn't believe my eyes, and that did not happen only once. It became a custom to see food in containers that did not belong in them.

When I was writing this book, the Holy Spirit reminded me of this scene and said, "That is the same thing that happens in people's lives."

I asked Him, "How so?"

He said, "Have you ever been labeled as something you are not? Have you ever been treated for what you look like from the outside, even though that was not who you truly are? Have people ever judged you by your external appearance without getting to know you deeper?"

I replied, "All the time."

This is exactly why George Eliot said, "Don't judge a book by its cover." There are so many factors to consider before we can give conclusions about somebody.

Before I go deeper in what God put in my spirit, let me define the word "label." According to the Oxford dictionary, a label is a classifying phrase or name applied to a person or thing for the purpose of giving more information or details. In the fashion industry, we have labels that give us information about a specific clothing, such as the brand, size, fabric, etc. In the food industry, we have labels that help us tell the difference between products, for example, when it comes to cooking, we ought to know how to differentiate between the different seasonings in our cabinet, otherwise we will use sugar instead of salt.

In life, people have labels. It might be labels that we attach to ourselves or labels that others have attached to us that reflect what they think about or how they consider us. Labels can be both negative or positive; true or wrong. Take a few minutes and think. If you were to label yourself using three words, what would they be?

_____

_____

_____

_____

_____

_____

Now that you have your words, let me tell you in advance that they might not be the same by the time you finish reading this book.

Labels are good; however, when they are not founded on good ground and are just based on assumptions and stereotypes, they become wrong and can have a negative effect on us and on the people around us. Everyone on this planet has been labeled for something they are not at least once in their life, either by themselves or by others.

113

In the book of Ruth, the Bible speaks of a woman named Naomi who lost her husband and both of her sons. She became so bitter because of what she went through. Naomi told her daughters-in-law to go back to their mother's house, but one of them, Ruth, refused and decided to stay with her. They both made their way back to Bethlehem. Once they arrived at the city, people, in the excitement of their arrival, started asking, "Is it really Naomi?" The Bible says Naomi forbade them from calling her like that. Instead, she told them to call her "Mara," for God, she said, has made her bitter (see Ruth 1:20). Naomi labeled herself and gave people the power to use that label on her. She didn't want to be called Naomi, which means sweetness, but Mara which means bitterness.

Aren't we all like Naomi at some point in our lives? We have grieved over people and things, and relationships have made us bitter and caused us to say negative things about ourselves. It does not matter what you have been through or what you might be going through right now, do not label yourself according to what you see or feel. Your words have power and vulnerability; brokenness, deception, hurt, and pain are the wrong places to pick a label from. Remember, you are not what you go through. There is a valid reason why God said to Jeremiah, *"Before you were formed in your mother's womb, I*

Your words have power and vulnerability; brokenness, deception, hurt, and pain are the wrong places to pick a label from.

knew you and I established you a prophet." (see Jeremiah 1:5). Our identity in Christ is set since eternity, and nothing on earth can change that. All we have to do is let Him reveal our identity to us every day. In fact, you were created with so much power to change the world, not to let the world change you.

The pain you go through does not make you weak, it unlocks the strength within you. If Joseph did not find himself behind bars, in a prison full of people who did what he did not do— with people he was supposed to rule over according to the vision God gave him and who were now cellmates—he wouldn't have unlocked the interpreter within him.

Allow God to change your labels today because, from the Old to the New Testament, He is known as a God who changes names and redefines labels. He changed Abram's name to Abraham, Sarai to Sarah, Jacob to Israel, Simon to Peter, and Saul to Paul. He will not only change your name, but He will also change your identity and your story. People and circumstances don't have the final say in your life, God does. If you let Him today, He will change your story. Like Rahab, known as the prostitute, because of God, she became one of the ancestors of Jesus Christ. God can turn things around for your good. Yes, you messed up. Yes, you are not who you are supposed to be or where you are supposed to be right now, but just one encounter with God and you will not be known for your weaknesses or mistakes by the generations that come after you. This book is God giving you an invitation to get a spiritual makeover. Let Him take those labels off you. Depression is not who you are. Sickness is not who you are.

Broken is not who you are. You are loved, blessed, and made whole.

At some point in my life, I labeled myself and allowed people to label me because of my mistakes and how ignorant I was about my identity. I have done things in my life that I will never be proud of. I messed up in so many areas of my life. I was broken, lost, and confused. I lost friends, and I settled for the labels people gave me.

Once I discovered my true identity in the Word of God, nothing and no one has ever made me less confident.

Once I became a Bible lover—once I learned to sit at the feet of Jesus—I realized that I had to lose everything to find myself.

When I look at myself in the mirror, I don't see what people say of me. I see the lioness, the queen, the masterpiece that is within me. Why? Because I allowed God to define me. You can do the same today, but first, **write down the labels you think you or the world have given you, good and bad:**

_____

_____

_____

_____

_____

Now pray this prayer with me:

Father, I humbly come into Your presence like Mary, the prostitute, who poured oil on Your feet. She ignored the label because she was in front of the one who gives an identity and changes stories. At Your feet I sit, and I surrender myself to You. You said in Your Word, "Come as you are." So, Jesus, I come with these labels, the ones I put on myself, and the ones the world has put on me. I pray that You will introduce me to me; the "me" You created, the "me" You gave a purpose. Change my name today, in the name of Your Son, Jesus Christ. Amen.

Sometimes you have to lose people and things to find yourself.

CHAPTER 13
IT'S A JOURNEY, AND IT STARTS NOW

A s much as we enjoy life, let us not forget that we only have one life here on earth. We might all be alive today, but no one has control over when and where it will end but God. It is important to take your life seriously. You have already wasted enough years living someone else's life. You have wasted your life living for the likes. You have already misused your time by lowering your boundaries to please people. You have already exhausted years believing the lies of the enemy concerning your life. Do not put your life on pause to watch others. It is time to get your identity back and live in the purpose God created you for, not tomorrow, not next month, not next year; the time is now.

One day I sat on my couch, scrolling through social media. 40% of the posts I saw were people dying, and questions started haunting me. I told myself, "God's plan is different for each person, and we never know when it is our time to go." The Psalmist David said, *"Teach us how to number our days so that we may apply our hearts to wisdom." (Psalm 90:12 - KJV).* I asked myself, "What if, according to God's plan for my life, I only have ten years left? Am I really doing what I'm supposed to do here on earth, or did I just waste almost ¾ of my life?" We don't all have the same amount of days on earth, so make every day count and live each day happily in God's purpose. As Christians, we should not be afraid of dying, but we should be afraid of not living well.

We should not fear dying but fear not living well.

Today, you get the chance to find yourself again, to find your identity in Christ and embrace it. Talk to the One who created you. Speak to Him through prayer and intimacy. Read and feed your mind on His Word daily and ask the Holy Spirit to help you on this journey to stay on track.

I am so excited about this journey you are about to embark on. It is one of confidence, happiness, peace, and purpose. Today, you get the chance to finally meet "you," and the next time someone asks you to "Tell Me About Yourself," you will not introduce anyone else but the true you with confidence and a smile.

Now that you know better, use the space below to answer the question, "Tell Me About Yourself?"

_____

_____

_____

_____

_____

_____

_____

_____

_____

_____

_____

_____

_____

_____

_____

_____

_____

_____

_____

_____

_____

CONCLUSION

I pray that this book opens your eyes to discover your true identity in Christ. I believe the next time you are asked to "Tell Me About Yourself," your answer will come with conviction.

Your life is too short to live someone else's script. God created you unique and valuable in His eyes. Despite the identity confusion and crisis this world is experiencing, have the courage to be different and to stand out. You do not have to blend in to be someone; your value does not depend on human approval. Your value depends on your identity in Christ. It is okay to be different. It is okay to not fit in. In fact, that is a sign that you are called for bigger things.

It doesn't matter who you have been for the past few years; you are not too lost or too messed up for God. Isaiah 43:18-

19a says, *"Do not remember the former things, nor consider the things of old. Behold, I will do a new thing." (NKJV)*. Jesus, through His blood, made all things new. Your life can be restored. Your heart can be made whole. All you need to do is surrender to Him and ask Him to introduce you to who He called you to be; the real "you."

I pray that God gives us the strength we need to stand firm in the truth of God. Let us not compromise ourselves to gain the world's attention. Mark 8:36 says, *" For what will it profit a man if he gains the whole world, and loses his own soul?" (NKJV)*. Think about it! Would you trade your eternity for temporary pleasures? You might live on earth for maybe one hundred years, but your life on earth will not be as long as your life after death.

Today, God is giving you an invitation to make things right. He wants to reveal your identity so you can live in the purpose He created you for. Don't forget, it is all in His Word. Read, meditate on it, and be it.

Welcome to the real "you."

ABOUT THE AUTHOR

Noella M. Mbulapey, also known as Marilla, is an ordained prophetess through City Harvest Network under the spiritual authority of Dr. Rod Parsley.

She is the overseer of Esther Generation Ministries, a platform with a mission to help generations discover and find their purpose in God through prayer, teachings of the Word of God, and the guidance of the Holy Spirit.

She is a gospel singer and is currently in the worship ministry of Harvest Music Live at World Harvest Church in Columbus, Ohio.

She graduated from the University of Texas at Arlington with a bachelor's degree in Political Science (Communication Minor) and an Associate of Science with Criminal Justice from Richland College in Dallas, TX. She is an entrepreneur and the CEO of the Qadash Companies. She is also a motivational speaker and coach who pushes people to their full potential and toward their destiny.